FATHOM BIBLE STUDIES

the passion

THE DEATH AND RESURRECTION OF JESUS

FATH◯M

A DEEP DIVE INTO THE STORY OF GOD

FATHOM: THE PASSION
THE DEATH AND RESURRECTION OF JESUS
STUDENT JOURNAL

Writer: Katie Heierman
Editor: Ben Howard
Designer: Keely Moore

Websites are constantly changing. Although the websites recommended in this resource were checked at the time this unit was developed, we recommend that you double-check all sites to verify that they are still live and that they are still suitable for students before doing the activity.

ISBN: 9781501838453

PACP10508943-01

17 18 19 20 21 22 23 24 25 26 — 10 9 8 7 6 5 4 3 2 1

MANUFACTURED IN THE UNITED STATES OF AMERICA

CONTENTS

About Fathom

Fathom.

It's such a big word. It feels endless and deep. It's the kind of word that feels like it should only be uttered by James Earl Jones with the bass turned all the way up.

Which means it's the perfect word to talk about a God who's infinite and awe-inspiring. It's also the perfect word for a book like the Bible that's filled with miracles and inspiration, but also wrestles with stories of violence and pain and loss.

The mission of *Fathom* is to dive deep into the story of God that we find in the Bible. You'll encounter Scriptures filled with inspiration and encouragement, and you'll also explore passages that are more complicated and challenging.

Each lesson will focus on one passage, but will also launch into the larger context of how God's story is being told through that passage. More importantly, each lesson will explore how God's story is intimately tied to our own stories, and how a God who is beyond our imagination can also be a God who loves us deeply and personally.

We invite you to wrestle with this and more as we dive deep into God's story.

Welcome

This book is yours. Or at least, it will be.

This book is designed to assist you as you explore, engage, and wrestle with everything that you'll experience over the next four weeks.

Each week during this study, this book will be filled with Scripture, activities, and questions to encourage and inspire you while you work your way through the Bible with your friends.

While we'll offer suggestions on how to use this journal, we want you to truly make it yours. Fill it with ideas and prayers. Take notes. Draw. Write poetry. Express yourself! Do whatever it is you need to do to help you remember what you've learned here.

Let this book be your canvas for creativity and self-expression. Let it be a place for honest questions and emotions that you may not feel comfortable expressing anywhere else, because at the end of this study, this book is yours.

You can use it to remember and reflect on what you learned, or you can use it to keep studying on your own, to keep questioning and exploring. We've included two sections at the end, "Takeaway" and "Explore More," to help you in that quest.

As you begin, we pray that you encounter the majesty and love of God through this study. We pray that you dive deep into the story of God and creation, and we pray that you find peace and hope in these lessons.

The Fathom 66 Bible Genre Guide

ENTER ZIP OR LOCATION [   ]

Stories ♡   TICKETS
★★★★★

Showtimes: Parts of Genesis, Joshua, Judges, Ruth, 1 Samuel,
2 Samuel, 1 Kings, 2 Kings, 1 Chronicles, 2 Chronicles, Ezra,
Nehemiah, Esther, Matthew, Mark, Luke, John, Acts

The Law ♡   TICKETS
★★★★★

Showtimes: Parts of Genesis, Exodus, Leviticus, Numbers,
Deuteronomy

Wisdom ♡   TICKETS
★★★★★

Showtimes: Job, Some Psalms, Proverbs, Ecclesiastes,
Song of Solomon, Lamentations, James

Psalms ♡   TICKETS
★★★★★

Showtimes: Psalms

The Prophets ♡   TICKETS
★★★★★

Showtimes: Isaiah, Jeremiah, Ezekiel, Hosea, Joel, Amos, Obadiah,
Jonah, Michah, Nahum, Habakkuk, Zephaniah, Haggai, Zechariah,
Malachi

Letters ♡   TICKETS
★★★★★

Showtimes: Romans, 1 Corinthians, 2 Corinthians, Galatians, Ephesians,
Philippians, Colossians, 1 Thessalonians, 2 Thessalonians, 1 Timothy, 2 Timothy,
Titus, Philemon, Hebrews, James, 1 Peter, 2 Peter, 1 John, 2 John, 3 John, Jude

Apocalyptic Writings ♡   TICKETS
★★★★★

Showtimes: Daniel, Revelation

The Fathom Bible Storylines

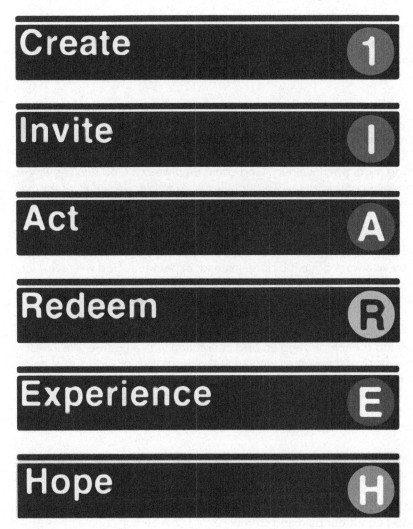

Create 1

Invite I

Act A

Redeem R

Experience E

Hope H

Introduction to The Passion

Background

We've all had one of *those* weeks—a week where our life is turned completely upside down from what it was when the week arrived. It may look like losing a job, the end of a relationship, or the death of a loved one.

When we study the Passion of Jesus, we are invited to journey with Jesus through one of those weeks. These Scriptures teach us important things about Jesus, and ultimately show us the true heart of God.

God hurts when we hurt. God cries when we cry. God rejoices when we are overcome with joy. Through Jesus' example, we see all of this and so much more.

As you embark on this study, I pray that you come to it with an attitude of expectation. Don't receive the story of Holy Week the same way you've always done it before. Instead, expect that God will reveal God's infinite love and grace to you in a fresh way. Dive into these Scriptures knowing that you will emerge with something new.

Over our time together, we'll explore Jesus' entry into Jerusalem, his visit to the temple, and an odd interaction with a fig tree. We'll hear the story of the woman who anointed Jesus with oil, and Jesus' own example of humility when he washed the feet of his followers. These are stories you've likely heard before, but think about what you might discover as you start to consider them as part of a single story and open your eyes to the nature of God in Jesus.

We'll also explore the pain that Jesus felt—the abandonment, betrayal, and loneliness that led up to his crucifixion. We'll see Jesus at his most vulnerable, crying out to God, and we'll be reminded that in this vulnerability, Jesus gives us an example of how we, too, can be open to God about our pain and sorrow.

I invite you to allow God to work in you during the next four weeks. Remember that Jesus, both fully God and fully human, walked through this life in the same way that you do. As we walk through this week with him, keep your eyes open for the ways Jesus shows us how God continues to be with God's created people.

Fathom Strategy for Reading and Understanding the Bible

"The Bible is written for us, but not to us."

This where we start on our quest. When we read the Bible, we have to constantly remember that the Bible is written for us, but not to us. Understanding the original context of the Bible helps us ask the right questions when interpreting Scripture.

For the first steps in our process, we need to understand how each passage we read functions in context and examine the historical background. When we read a passage, we should ask questions about the era, location, and culture of the original audience, as well as how a particular writing relates to the larger narrative of the Bible. This strategy not only helps us understand a passage's primary meaning, it also gives us guidance on how to translate that meaning into our specific circumstances today.

Deep Cleaning

Summary

Today you'll explore and reflect on Jesus' arrival into Jerusalem and explore the ways that Jesus' arrival disrupted normal religious practices of the time.

Overview

- **Sync** with the idea that thinking and acting differently can make things uncomfortable for others.
- **Tour** through the Gospel Scriptures covering the entry to Jerusalem, Jesus cleansing the temple, and the cursing of the fig tree.
- **Reveal** how the Scripture connects to you and how you can create change in the midst of opposition.
- **Build** a new understanding of the story of Jesus' entry into Jerusalem by creating a comic strip depicting the Gospel narrative.
- **After** the lesson, share what you've learned with others by putting these lessons into practice.

Anchor Point

- Matthew 21:10-11—*And when Jesus entered Jerusalem, the whole city was stirred up. "Who is this?" they asked. The crowds answered, "It's the prophet Jesus from Nazareth in Galilee."*

Flipping Out

What was the most frustrating part of this game?

Have you ever been in a situation where you were trying to do one thing, but it felt like others were doing the complete opposite?

Honey, Do You Love Me?

If you cracked, what made you smile?

Did you get a little nervous or feel awkward? Why?

Matthew 21:1-22

When they approached Jerusalem and came to Bethphage on the Mount of Olives, Jesus gave two disciples a task. He said to them, "Go into the village over there. As soon as you enter, you will find a donkey tied up and a colt with it. Untie them and bring them to me. If anybody says anything to you, say that the Lord needs it." He sent them off right away. Now this happened to fulfill what the prophet said, *Say to Daughter Zion, "Look, your king is coming to you, humble and riding on a donkey, and on a colt the donkey's offspring."* The disciples went and did just as Jesus had ordered them. They brought the donkey and the colt and laid their clothes on them. Then he sat on them.

Now a large crowd spread their clothes on the road. Others cut palm branches off the trees and spread them on the road. The crowds in front of him and behind him shouted, "*Hosanna* to the Son of David! *Blessings on the one who comes in the name of the Lord! Hosanna* in the highest!" And when Jesus entered Jerusalem, the whole city was stirred up. "Who is this?" they asked. The crowds answered, "It's the prophet Jesus from Nazareth in Galilee."

Then Jesus went into the temple and threw out all those who were selling and buying there. He pushed over the tables used for currency exchange and the chairs of those who sold doves. He said to them, "It's written, *My house will be called a house of prayer.* But you've made it a hideout for crooks."

People who were blind and lame came to Jesus in the temple, and he healed them. But when the chief priests and legal experts saw the amazing things he was doing and the children shouting in the temple, "*Hosanna* to the Son of David!" they were angry. They said to Jesus, "Do you hear what these children are saying?"

Matthew 21:1-22 (continued)

"Yes," he answered. "Haven't you ever read, *From the mouths of babies and infants you've arranged praise for yourself?*" Then he left them and went out of the city to Bethany and spent the night there.

Early in the morning as Jesus was returning to the city, he was hungry. He saw a fig tree along the road, but when he came to it, he found nothing except leaves. Then he said to it, "You'll never again bear fruit!" The fig tree dried up at once.

When the disciples saw it, they were amazed. "How did the fig tree dry up so fast?" they asked.

Jesus responded, "I assure you that if you have faith and don't doubt, you will not only do what was done to the fig tree. You will even say to this mountain, 'Be lifted up and thrown into the lake.' And it will happen. If you have faith, you will receive whatever you pray for."

Key Points

1) _____

2) _____

3) _____

4) _____

5) _____

Mark 11:1-19

When Jesus and his followers approached Jerusalem, they came to Bethphage and Bethany at the Mount of Olives. Jesus gave two disciples a task, saying to them, "Go into the village over there. As soon as you enter it, you will find tied up there a colt that no one has ridden. Untie it and bring it here. If anyone says to you, 'Why are you doing this?' say, 'Its master needs it, and he will send it back right away.' "

They went and found a colt tied to a gate outside on the street, and they untied it. Some people standing around said to them, "What are you doing, untying the colt?" They told them just what Jesus said, and they left them alone. They brought the colt to Jesus and threw their clothes upon it, and he sat on it. Many people spread out their clothes on the road while others spread branches cut from the fields. Those in front of him and those following were shouting, "*Hosanna! Blessings on the one who comes in the name of the Lord!* Blessings on the coming kingdom of our ancestor David! Hosanna in the highest!" Jesus entered Jerusalem and went into the temple. After he looked around at everything, because it was already late in the evening, he returned to Bethany with the Twelve.

The next day, after leaving Bethany, Jesus was hungry. From far away, he noticed a fig tree in leaf, so he went to see if he could find anything on it. When he came to it, he found nothing except leaves, since it wasn't the season for figs. So he said to it, "No one will ever again eat your fruit!" His disciples heard this.

Mark 11:1-19 (continued)

They came into Jerusalem. After entering the temple, he threw out those who were selling and buying there. He pushed over the tables used for currency exchange and the chairs of those who sold doves. He didn't allow anyone to carry anything through the temple. He taught them, "Hasn't it been written, *My house will be called a house of prayer for all nations*? But you've turned it into *a hideout for crooks*." The chief priests and legal experts heard this and tried to find a way to destroy him. They regarded him as dangerous because the whole crowd was enthralled at his teaching. When it was evening, Jesus and his disciples went outside the city.

Key Points

1) _____

2) _____

3) _____

4) _____

5) _____

6) _____

Luke 19:29-48

As Jesus came to Bethphage and Bethany on the Mount of Olives, he gave two disciples a task. He said, "Go into the village over there. When you enter it, you will find tied up there a colt that no one has ever ridden. Untie it and bring it here. If someone asks, 'Why are you untying it?' just say, 'Its master needs it.' " Those who had been sent found it exactly as he had said.

As they were untying the colt, its owners said to them, "Why are you untying the colt?"

They replied, "Its master needs it." They brought it to Jesus, threw their clothes on the colt, and lifted Jesus onto it. As Jesus rode along, they spread their clothes on the road.

As Jesus approached the road leading down from the Mount of Olives, the whole throng of his disciples began rejoicing. They praised God with a loud voice because of all the mighty things they had seen. They said,

> "Blessings on the king who comes in the name of the Lord.
> Peace in heaven and glory in the highest heavens."

Some of the Pharisees from the crowd said to Jesus, "Teacher, scold your disciples! Tell them to stop!"

He answered, "I tell you, if they were silent, the stones would shout."

Luke 19:29-48 (continued)

As Jesus came to the city and observed it, he wept over it. He said, "If only you knew on this of all days the things that lead to peace. But now they are hidden from your eyes. The time will come when your enemies will build fortifications around you, encircle you, and attack you from all sides. They will crush you completely, you and the people within you. They won't leave one stone on top of another within you, because you didn't recognize the time of your gracious visit from God."

When Jesus entered the temple, he threw out those who were selling things there. He said to them, "It's written, *My house will be a house of prayer*, but you have made it a hideout for crooks."

Jesus was teaching daily in the temple. The chief priests, the legal experts, and the foremost leaders among the people were seeking to kill him. However, they couldn't find a way to do it because all the people were enthralled with what they heard.

Key Points

1) _____

2) _____

3) _____

4) _____

5) _____

6) _____

7) _____

John 12:12-19

The next day the great crowd that had come for the festival heard that Jesus was coming to Jerusalem. They took palm branches and went out to meet him. They shouted,

> "Hosanna!
> *Blessings on the one who comes*
> *in the name of the Lord!*
> Blessings on the king of Israel!"

Jesus found a young donkey and sat on it, just as it is written,

> *Don't be afraid, Daughter Zion.*
> *Look! Your king is coming,*
> *sitting on a donkey's colt.*

His disciples didn't understand these things at first. After he was glorified, they remembered that these things had been written about him and that they had done these things to him.

The crowd who had been with him when he called Lazarus out of the tomb and raised him from the dead were testifying about him. That's why the crowd came to meet him, because they had heard about this miraculous sign that he had done. Therefore, the Pharisees said to each other, "See! You've accomplished nothing! Look! The whole world is following him!"

TOUR

FATH●M

Key Points

1) _____

2) _____

3) _____

4) _____

5) _____

Spend the next few minutes responding to the following questions. You don't need to answer all of them. Focus on the ones that most intrigue you.

Does the "grand entrance" look like what you'd imagine a grand entrance to look like?

Were you surprised to read how Jesus cleared out the temple? Why?

Why do you think Jesus got mad at and cursed a fig tree? What could the fig tree have symbolized?

What things would you like to see happen in your church or community that you feel are resisted by adults or church leaders? What are some ways you could try to convince them about why your ideas are important?

BUILD   FATH⬤M

Use the framework below to sketch out ideas for a comic depicting Jesus' entrance into Jerusalem. For example, the first frame might be Jesus telling the disciples to get the donkey or maybe Jesus entering the city.

Be as creative as you can!

AFTER

Use your phone to take a picture of what you wrote in the Reveal section today. Revisit it over the course of this week.

The Change You Want to See

This week find a video or image that conveys the kind of change you want to see happen in the world. Make sure it's something real and that it's something positive. Then share it with all your friends and followers on social media.

Family Surprise

Sometime this week, do something to surprise your parents, siblings, or other family members in a good way. For example, wash the dishes or take out the trash without being asked. Try to give as many positive surprises as you can this week to create positive change in your home.

What are some things you could do this week to surprise your family in a positive way?

1) _____

2) _____

3) _____

PRAYER FATH●M

LEADER: God, open our eyes.

YOUTH: Let us see your passion.

LEADER: God, mold our hearts.

YOUTH: Let us become who you've called us to be.

LEADER: God, give us strength.

YOUTH: Let us stand firm in the face of opposition.

LEADER: We love you.

YOUTH: We love you.

ALL: Amen.

Presence

Summary

This lesson highlights the importance of love in community. This love is particularly evident in Jesus' interactions with his disciples during the Last Supper and the events leading up to it.

Overview

- **Sync** with the importance of presence by recognizing how we rely on others.
- **Tour** through the events leading up to and including the Last Supper through a series of experiential readings.
- **Reveal** another side of the familiar stories of the anointing of Jesus and the Last Supper by re-envisioning them in new contexts.
- **Build** on these revelations by using your creative abilities to tell the story of Jesus and his followers.
- **After** the lesson, try one of the activities and be present with others this week.

Anchor Point

- John 13:19-20—*I'm telling you this now, before it happens, so that when it does happen you will believe that I Am. I assure you that whoever receives someone I send receives me, and whoever receives me receives the one who sent me.*

Better Together

STEP 1: Position your chairs in a tight circle, facing inward.

STEP 2: Have four of your group members sit down in the chair sideways with their feet touching the ground. Make sure everyone is facing counterclockwise.

STEP 3: One at a time, lie backward, resting your head on the legs of the person behind you.

STEP 4: Once everyone is lying backward, the fifth person should VERY carefully remove the chairs from under each person one at a time. You may need to adjust so you're resting your full weight on your legs and the lap of the person behind you.

What was it like when the chair was taken out from under you? When you heard that you'd be forming a human table, did you believe it would happen?

Our lesson today is about the importance of being together. This activity shows us that we can do more together than we can alone.

Drawing in the Dark

Which drawings look the closest to the objects the blindfolded students were given? Which process led to more accurate drawings?

Sometimes the best way to help someone understand something is to let them experience it for themselves. Our lesson today explores that further.

FATH●M

The Anointing—Matthew 26:6-13

When Jesus was at Bethany visiting the house of Simon, who had a skin disease, a woman came to him with a vase made of alabaster containing very expensive perfume. She poured it on Jesus' head while he was sitting at dinner. Now when the disciples saw it they were angry and said, "Why this waste? This perfume could have been sold for a lot of money and given to the poor."

But Jesus knew what they were thinking. He said, "Why do you make trouble for the woman? She's done a good thing for me. You always have the poor with you, but you won't always have me. By pouring this perfume over my body she's prepared me to be buried. I tell you the truth that wherever in the whole world this good news is announced, what she's done will also be told in memory of her."

What did you experience at this station?

_____

_____

_____

_____

_____

The Foot-Washing—John 13:1-20

Before the Festival of Passover, Jesus knew that his time had come to leave this world and go to the Father. Having loved his own who were in the world, he loved them fully.

Jesus and his disciples were sharing the evening meal. The devil had already provoked Judas, Simon Iscariot's son, to betray Jesus. Jesus knew the Father had given everything into his hands and that he had come from God and was returning to God. So he got up from the table and took off his robes. Picking up a linen towel, he tied it around his waist. Then he poured water into a washbasin and began to wash the disciples' feet, drying them with the towel he was wearing. When Jesus came to Simon Peter, Peter said to him, "Lord, are you going to wash my feet?"

Jesus replied, "You don't understand what I'm doing now, but you will understand later."

"No!" Peter said. "You will never wash my feet!"

Jesus replied, "Unless I wash you, you won't have a place with me."

Simon Peter said, "Lord, not only my feet but also my hands and my head!"

Jesus responded, "Those who have bathed need only to have their feet washed, because they are completely clean. You disciples are clean, but not every one of you." He knew who would betray him. That's why he said, "Not every one of you is clean."

The Foot-Washing—John 13:1-20 (continued)

After he washed the disciples' feet, he put on his robes and returned to his place at the table. He said to them, "Do you know what I've done for you? You call me 'Teacher' and 'Lord,' and you speak correctly, because I am. If I, your Lord and teacher, have washed your feet, you too must wash each other's feet. I have given you an example: just as I have done, you also must do. I assure you, servants aren't greater than their master, nor are those who are sent greater than the one who sent them. Since you know these things, you will be happy if you do them. I'm not speaking about all of you. I know those whom I've chosen. But this is to fulfill the scripture, *The one who eats my bread has turned against me.*

"I'm telling you this now, before it happens, so that when it does happen you will believe that I Am. I assure you that whoever receives someone I send receives me, and whoever receives me receives the one who sent me."

What did you experience at this station?

_____

_____

_____

_____

_____

The Last Supper—Mark 14:10-26

Judas Iscariot, one of the Twelve, went to the chief priests to give Jesus up to them. When they heard it, they were delighted and promised to give him money. So he started looking for an opportunity to turn him in.

On the first day of the Festival of Unleavened Bread, when the Passover lamb was sacrificed, the disciples said to Jesus, "Where do you want us to prepare for you to eat the Passover meal?"

He sent two of his disciples and said to them, "Go into the city. A man carrying a water jar will meet you. Follow him. Wherever he enters, say to the owner of the house, 'The teacher asks, "Where is my guest room where I can eat the Passover meal with my disciples?"' He will show you a large room upstairs already furnished. Prepare for us there." The disciples left, came into the city, found everything just as he had told them, and they prepared the Passover meal.

That evening, Jesus arrived with the Twelve. During the meal, Jesus said, "I assure you that one of you will betray me—someone eating with me."

Deeply saddened, they asked him, one by one, "It's not me, is it?"

Jesus answered, "It's one of the Twelve, one who is dipping bread with me into this bowl. The Human One goes to his death just as it is written about him. But how terrible it is for that person who betrays the Human One! It would have been better for him if he had never been born."

The Last Supper—Mark 14:10-26 (continued)

While they were eating, Jesus took bread, blessed it, broke it, and gave it to them, and said, "Take; this is my body." He took a cup, gave thanks, and gave it to them, and they all drank from it. He said to them, "This is my blood of the covenant, which is poured out for many. I assure you that I won't drink wine again until that day when I drink it in a new way in God's kingdom." After singing songs of praise, they went out to the Mount of Olives.

What did you experience at this station?

_____

_____

_____

_____

_____

The Table—1 Corinthians 11:23-26

I received a tradition from the Lord, which I also handed on to you: on the night on which he was betrayed, the Lord Jesus took bread. After giving thanks, he broke it and said, "This is my body, which is for you; do this to remember me." He did the same thing with the cup, after they had eaten, saying, "This cup is the new covenant in my blood. Every time you drink it, do this to remember me." Every time you eat this bread and drink this cup, you broadcast the death of the Lord until he comes.

What did you experience at this station?

_____

_____

_____

_____

_____

REVEAL FATH●M

For the next few minutes, imagine what would happen in the following scenarios and journal about how they would make you feel.

Scenario One

Youth group is about to start, and everyone is sitting in a circle waiting for your youth leader to begin the lesson. All of a sudden, a strange woman enters the room and wordlessly begins to pour essential oil on the feet of your youth leader and washes them with a towel. As this happens, your youth leader continues with the lesson completely unfazed.

What would you say? Would it make you uncomfortable? Why?

Scenario Two

It's Christmas dinner, and you're gathered together with your best friends and closest family. As the meal is about to begin, the host begins to talk about his or her coming death and asks you to think of him or her each time you gather together to eat this specific meal in the future.

How would you respond? Would it make you uncomfortable? Why?

BUILD FATH●M

Using your experiences and reflections from this lesson, create your own vision of what you think the Last Supper was like. Be creative and try to depict it differently than the ways you've seen it before.

You could paint a picture or write a song. Maybe you want to set it in the future or show it from the perspective of one of the disciples. Make sure it showcases something you feel is important about this event.

Different Dinner Tables

This week take some time at lunch to ask your friends what a regular weeknight dinner looks like at their house. What do they eat? Who is there? Do they enjoy it or do they wish it were different? Think about their experience in relation to what goes on at your home.

Being Present

Nursing-home residents and people who are homebound can feel very lonely, especially if they no longer have family. Ask your leader or the church office for a list of names and addresses of church members who live in nursing homes or can no longer get out of their homes. Write letters or send cards to them. Invite your recipients to write back to you. You might even make a new friend!

#PassionPresence

Take a picture with your family or group of friends and share it on social media along with your feelings about what it means to be present with them in tough times. Use #PassionPresence to tag your picture.

PRAYER FATH●M

Pray the following prayer silently to yourself:

God, just like Jesus came to be present with us, help me be present with others. Especially with

---

When the leader begins, say the following out loud:

ALL: Therefore, let's draw near to God with a genuine heart, with the certainty that our faith gives us, since our hearts are sprinkled clean and our bodies are washed pure with water.

Amen.

Betrayal

Summary

In this lesson, you will explore disappointment and betrayal from those you love and make steps toward forgiveness and peace.

Overview

- **Sync** with the disappointment and frustration that happens when people don't do what they should through a group activity.
- **Tour** through Matthew 26 to explore the concepts of friendship, peace, and forgiveness, in spite of betrayal and disappointment.
- **Reveal** to each other scenarios where forgiveness is needed and advise each other on how to proceed in light of Jesus' example.
- **Build** a "peace treaty" for an area of conflict in your life to help you find tangible ways to pursue peace.
- **After** the lesson, choose one of the activities challenging you to show forgiveness this week to both yourself and others.

Anchor Point

- Matthew 26:50—*But Jesus said to him, "Friend, do what you came to do."*

Stand Up!

If you had a hard time with this activity, what made it so frustrating? Why?

Storytelling

What was your original sentence?

What did it end up saying?

Did things turn out as expected?

Why do you think that happened?

Things can work really well when we work together, but it can be frustrating and disheartening if one person works against the group. Today we're going to explore this disappointment.

Kneel as the first passage is read. Consider what is going through the minds of the disciples in this passage.

Matthew 26:36-46

Then Jesus went with his disciples to a place called Gethsemane. He said to the disciples, "Stay here while I go and pray over there." When he took Peter and Zebedee's two sons, he began to feel sad and anxious. Then he said to them, "I'm very sad. It's as if I'm dying. Stay here and keep alert with me." Then he went a short distance farther and fell on his face and prayed, "My Father, if it's possible, take this cup of suffering away from me. However—not what I want but what you want."

He came back to the disciples and found them sleeping. He said to Peter, "Couldn't you stay alert one hour with me? Stay alert and pray so that you won't give in to temptation. The spirit is eager, but the flesh is weak." A second time he went away and prayed, "My Father, if it's not possible that this cup be taken away unless I drink it, then let it be what you want."

Again he came and found them sleeping. Their eyes were heavy with sleep. But he left them and again went and prayed the same words for the third time. Then he came to his disciples and said to them, "Will you sleep and rest all night? Look, the time has come for the Human One to be betrayed into the hands of sinners. Get up. Let's go. Look, here comes my betrayer."

Why do you think Jesus wanted his disciples to stay awake and pray with him?

TOUR FATH●M

While this passage is read, focus on the picture at the front of the room. Think about what you see in the picture that is also in the Scripture being read.

Matthew 26:47-56

While Jesus was still speaking, Judas, one of the Twelve, came. With him was a large crowd carrying swords and clubs. They had been sent by the chief priests and elders of the people. His betrayer had given them a sign: "Arrest the man I kiss." Just then he came to Jesus and said, "Hello, Rabbi." Then he kissed him.

But Jesus said to him, "Friend, do what you came to do." Then they came and grabbed Jesus and arrested him.

One of those with Jesus reached for his sword. Striking the high priest's slave, he cut off his ear. Then Jesus said to him, "Put the sword back into its place. All those who use the sword will die by the sword. Or do you think that I'm not able to ask my Father and he will send to me more than twelve battle groups of angels right away? But if I did that, how would the scriptures be fulfilled that say this must happen?" Then Jesus said to the crowds, "Have you come with swords and clubs to arrest me, like a thief? Day after day, I sat in the temple teaching, but you didn't arrest me. But all this has happened so that what the prophets said in the scriptures might be fulfilled." Then all the disciples left Jesus and ran away.

What parts of the Scripture do you see in this painting of the event? Is this how you've pictured Jesus' betrayal? What did you think would be different?

As this passage is read, underline the responses and actions of Jesus. Consider what was going through Jesus' mind as this was all happening.

Matthew 26:57-68

Those who arrested Jesus led him to Caiaphas the high priest. The legal experts and the elders had gathered there. Peter followed him from a distance until he came to the high priest's courtyard. He entered that area and sat outside with the officers to see how it would turn out.

The chief priests and the whole council were looking for false testimony against Jesus so that they could put him to death. They didn't find anything they could use from the many false witnesses who were willing to come forward. But finally they found two who said, "This man said, 'I can destroy God's temple and rebuild it in three days.'"

Then the high priest stood and said to Jesus, "Aren't you going to respond to the testimony these people have brought against you?"

But Jesus was silent.

The high priest said, "By the living God, I demand that you tell us whether you are the Christ, God's Son."

"You said it," Jesus replied. "But I say to you that from now on you'll see *the Human One sitting on the right side of the Almighty and coming on the heavenly clouds.*"

Matthew 26:57-68 (continued)

Then the high priest tore his clothes and said, "He's insulting God! Why do we need any more witnesses? Look, you've heard his insult against God. What do you think?"

And they answered, "He deserves to die!" Then they spit in his face and beat him. They hit him and said, "Prophesy for us, Christ! Who hit you?"

How did Jesus act in the face of these accusations? What did he say? Why do you think he responded this way?

You're all going to act out the last passage together. Think about what Peter is going through as all this happens.

Matthew 26:69-75

Narrator: Meanwhile, Peter was sitting outside in the courtyard. A servant woman came and said to him,

Servant woman: You were also with Jesus the Galilean.

Narrator: But he denied it in front of all of them, saying,

Peter: I don't know what you are talking about.

Narrator: When he went over to the gate, another woman saw him and said to those who were there,

Woman by the gate: This man was with Jesus, the man from Nazareth.

Narrator: With a solemn pledge, he denied it again, saying,

Peter: I don't know the man.

Narrator: A short time later, those standing there came and said to Peter,

All: You must be one of them. The way you talk gives you away.

Narrator: Then he cursed and swore,

Peter: I don't know the man!

Narrator: At that very moment, the rooster crowed. Peter remembered Jesus' words, "Before the rooster crows you will deny me three times." And Peter went out and cried uncontrollably.

Have you ever denied something when you found yourself in an uncomfortable situation?

Considering all he had endured up to this point, are you surprised by the way Jesus responded? Do you think you'd be able to respond in the same way?

Matthew 26:50

But Jesus said to him, "Friend, do what you came to do." Then they came and grabbed Jesus and arrested him.

Do you think Jesus would have forgiven Judas if Judas had asked for it? Why or why not?

You'll need a partner for this activity.

Your Story

Write out a scenario from the recent past where someone hurt you or you hurt someone else. Focus on the emotions and the way each of you has responded.

Trade Student Journals with your partner.

Their Advice

Read what your partner wrote and respond below with advice based on the example of Jesus from our lesson today. How can we apply that thinking toward making peace in this situation?

BUILD FATH●M

Create a peace treaty. This can be for two friends, family members, groups of people, or even countries, if you so choose.

Remember, peace works two ways. Someone has to extend the peace, and the other has to accept it. Both sides will need to move toward peace together.

Who is involved in your peace treaty?

_____

Why are they fighting?

_____

_____

What will each side give up to move toward peace?

_____

_____

_____

When and where will they meet to sign this treaty?

_____

_____

The Treaty of Peace

between

_____

and

_____

to resolve their dispute about

_____

_____

The parties agree to

_____

_____

_____

Signed at _____

on _____

Peace With Others

Think of someone you have often had a contentious relationship with—maybe it's a parent or a teacher or a classmate. This week do a kind act for this person or send a note saying why you appreciate her or him. Don't look for attention; just do it because it's a good thing to do.

Who can you do a kind act for this week?

1) _____

2) _____

3) _____

Peace With Yourself

This week sit down for fifteen or twenty minutes and write yourself a letter of forgiveness. In the future, whenever you start to feel angry at yourself for one reason or another, pull out your letter and remind yourself of this forgiveness.

Peace From God

This week look for signs of God's forgiveness and mercy in the world around you. When you find one, take a picture and post it on social media. Use #PassionPeace to highlight what you've found.

PRAYER FATHOM

God,

We all know how hard it is to forgive someone for hurting us. And we all know how it feels to hurt someone else. Help us remember what both of those things feel like when we are faced with difficult situations. May we always act in the way that shows your love.

Amen.

Alone

Summary

Today you'll explore the topics of pain and abandonment. You'll also explore how to respond with love to those who suffer.

Overview

- **Sync** with the concept that we are stronger when we work together instead of isolating ourselves.
- **Tour** through the story of Jesus' trial and execution to understand how Jesus dealt with suffering.
- **Reveal** how you relate to the suffering and vulnerability of Jesus by reflecting on your own experiences of suffering.
- **Build** a clay representation of ways you can serve those who are suffering or alone.
- **After** the lesson, consider the needs of others and think about how you can show them love this week.

Anchor Point

- Luke 23:34—*Jesus said, "Father, forgive them, for they don't know what they're doing."*

Hula Roundup

Your goal is to get all the items inside of your Hula-Hoop. The game is over when all of the items are in one hoop. You can get items at any time, and you can even take them out of another team's hoop.

Did you find this activity frustrating? Why was it so difficult?

What do you think the point of the activity was?

Today we're going to explore what it feels like to be alone and what we can do as a community to work together and support one another.

Make Me a Sandwich

What hints would you give to help a blindfolded person make a peanut-butter-and-jelly sandwich?

_____

_____

_____

_____

_____

Which attempt worked best? Why did it work better? Was it hard to watch your friend try to make a sandwich blindfolded without being able to help?

Today we're going to explore what it feels like to be alone and what we can do as a community to make sure we support one another in tough times.

Matthew 27:17-24

When the crowd had come together, Pilate asked them, "Whom would you like me to release to you, Jesus Barabbas or Jesus who is called Christ?" He knew that the leaders of the people had handed him over because of jealousy.

While he was serving as judge, his wife sent this message to him, "Leave that righteous man alone. I've suffered much today in a dream because of him."

But the chief priests and the elders persuaded the crowds to ask for Barabbas and kill Jesus. The governor said, "Which of the two do you want me to release to you?"

"Barabbas," they replied.

Pilate said, "Then what should I do with Jesus who is called Christ?"

They all said, "Crucify him!"

But he said, "Why? What wrong has he done?"

They shouted even louder, "Crucify him!"

Pilate saw that he was getting nowhere and that a riot was starting. So he took water and washed his hands in front of the crowd. "I'm innocent of this man's blood," he said. "It's your problem."

Have you ever been in a situation where you didn't act and wished later that you had? What changed?

Dive Deeper

If you are neutral in situations of injustice, you have chosen the side of the oppressor. If an elephant has its foot on the tail of a mouse and you say that you are neutral, the mouse will not appreciate your neutrality.

—Archbishop Desmond Tutu, South-African civil rights leader

What does this quotation mean to you? Do you think Pilate considered the ramifications his choice would have for Jesus and the world?

Luke 23:32-43

Circle the verse that sticks out to you most.

They also led two other criminals to be executed with Jesus. When they arrived at the place called The Skull, they crucified him, along with the criminals, one on his right and the other on his left. Jesus said, "Father, forgive them, for they don't know what they're doing." They drew lots as a way of dividing up his clothing.

The people were standing around watching, but the leaders sneered at him, saying, "He saved others. Let him save himself if he really is the Christ sent from God, the chosen one."

The soldiers also mocked him. They came up to him, offering him sour wine and saying, "If you really are the king of the Jews, save yourself." Above his head was a notice of the formal charge against him. It read "This is the king of the Jews."

One of the criminals hanging next to Jesus insulted him: "Aren't you the Christ? Save yourself and us!"

Responding, the other criminal spoke harshly to him, "Don't you fear God, seeing that you've also been sentenced to die? We are rightly condemned, for we are receiving the appropriate sentence for what we did. But this man has done nothing wrong." Then he said, "Jesus, remember me when you come into your kingdom."

Jesus replied, "I assure you that today you will be with me in paradise."

Have you ever been in a situation where you felt the need to prove yourself, but you knew that would make things worse?

Mark 15:33-39

From noon until three in the afternoon the whole earth was dark. At three, Jesus cried out with a loud shout, *"Eloi, eloi, lama sabachthani,"* which means, "My God, my God, why have you left me?"

After hearing him, some standing there said, "Look! He's calling Elijah!" Someone ran, filled a sponge with sour wine, and put it on a pole. He offered it to Jesus to drink, saying, "Let's see if Elijah will come to take him down." But Jesus let out a loud cry and died.

The curtain of the sanctuary was torn in two from top to bottom. When the centurion, who stood facing Jesus, saw how he died, he said, "This man was certainly God's Son."

What do you think when you see people share their deepest emotions? Does it make you uncomfortable? Why or why not?

Over the last few weeks, we've been learning about the experiences of Jesus leading up to his crucifixion and death. We've been learning about his experience of suffering on our behalf.

Take a few moments and journal about what it has meant to you to reflect on Jesus' experience. Ask yourself what it's felt like when you've gone through suffering. What did it feel like when you seemed to be alone or abandoned?

Trade journals with a partner.

Read what your partner has written in her or his reflection.

Write a prayer that will help your partner remember what she or he has learned from studying the Passion.

BUILD

FATH●M

Spend a few minutes thinking about the things in the world that cause so much suffering that you can't ignore them. Think about the things you want to help change.

Take the piece of clay you've been given and shape it into something that represents what you feel called to change.

I used my clay to make _____

_____

This represents my passion to _____

_____

Feel Their Feelings

This week when you feel hurt or upset, pause and think of someone else who might be feeling a similar way. Send a text or leave a note to encourage that person.

Who are some people you know who are having a tough time right now?

1) _____

2) _____

3) _____

Homemade Sacrifice

Jesus was aware of the needs of those around him. In fact, he sacrificed to meet so many of their needs. This week think of something you can sacrifice at home to make life easier for someone in your family.

What is one thing you could sacrifice at home this week?

_____

Not Alone

A lot of people use social media so that they will feel more connected to their friends and not feel lonely. This week go out of your way to comment on the social media posts of a friend or classmate you don't typically interact with to assure this person that you are thinking of him or her and they are not alone.

Who are some friends or classmates you could encourage on social media this week?

1) _____

2) _____

3) _____

But now, LORD, you are our father.
We are the clay, and you are our potter.
All of us are the work of your hand. — Isaiah 64:8

Lord, shape us so we may bring your loving passion to this world.

Amen.

A Little More . . .

Q: Why did Pilate offer to release a prisoner to the crowd, and who was this Barabbas guy anyway?

A: According to the Gospels, there was a tradition that the Roman authorities would release a prisoner at Passover every year. It's unknown whether it originated as a Jewish or a Roman custom, but it was likely viewed as a goodwill offering on both sides.

Barabbas in particular was an ironic choice for such a release. According to the Gospel of Luke, Barabbas had committed murder as part of an uprising against the Roman government and was in prison for treason, the same crime of which Jesus was accused. Scholars think that Barabbas might have been a member of the Zealots or the sicarii (dagger-men), both of which were armed groups that sought to overthrow the Roman occupiers.

The crowd's desire for Barabbas appears to point to their desire for a physical kingdom, even if it requires violence rather than the peaceful heavenly kingdom offered by Jesus.

Takeaway

Over the past few weeks, we've explored Jesus' journey to the cross. We've explored what he thought and felt, and tried to connect with our own thoughts and emotions to see how Jesus' experience could connect with our own. Jesus did much more for us than give his life. All of the things that led Jesus to that climactic moment have also changed the way we live in the world today.

Think about it. If Jesus had just been born, lived, and then died, would we have been impacted as deeply? No! The depth and truth of Jesus' death is found in what he taught us during his life and what that death meant as a result.

Jesus didn't settle for the status quo. In our first lesson, we saw Jesus disrupt traditions and social expectations. He rode into Jerusalem on a lowly donkey and was greeted with elation. He went into the temple, which had become a marketplace, and cleansed it to make it a house of prayer once again. Jesus forced the people of God to confront their errors and to once again bear the image and love of God.

We saw Jesus continue to disrupt these social expectations in our second lesson as he welcomed the woman who anointed his feet with perfume and humbled himself to wash the feet of his disciples. This was the act of a servant. Jesus carried himself in a way that was holy, and in him we see that loving and serving others is far more important than putting on a show for others.

This theme continued in our third lesson when Jesus revealed his vulnerability in the garden. He is in distress and needs the support of his friends, but they cannot stay awake. Then when Judas betrays him, Jesus still refers to him as a friend. He continues to encounter difficult situations and respond to them in unusual ways that show how the kingdom of God is different than the kingdoms of earth.

In the betrayals of both Judas and Peter, we are shown that the love of Jesus is even greater than pain or betrayal. Jesus knew that they weren't perfect, but he still loved them. The grace Jesus shows his disciples can serve as an example of the grace available to us, despite our past mistakes.

Even in our final lesson—one that was filled with darkness, pain, and fear—Jesus continues to stand firm in love. It is through this example that we can find courage and commit to do what God has called us to do. It is through the atonement given to us by Jesus that we are made new in God's eyes. We are called to live as Jesus lived, no longer in darkness.

Moving forward from this study, may you embrace the ways God is leading you to change the status quo, remind the world of this incredible grace, and seek to become one with the life and love of Jesus.

Explore More

John 12:3-8

Then Mary took an extraordinary amount, almost three-quarters of a pound, of very expensive perfume made of pure nard. She anointed Jesus' feet with it, then wiped his feet dry with her hair. The house was filled with the aroma of the perfume. Judas Iscariot, one of his disciples (the one who was about to betray him), complained, "This perfume was worth a year's wages! Why wasn't it sold and the money given to the poor?" (He said this not because he cared about the poor but because he was a thief. He carried the money bag and would take what was in it.)

Then Jesus said, "Leave her alone. This perfume was to be used in preparation for my burial, and this is how she has used it. You will always have the poor among you, but you won't always have me."

Application

• Mary doesn't shy away from Jesus, but does what she can to get even closer. This shows us the devotion we are to have when we serve Christ. Even when some that were close with Jesus questioned what she was doing, she still stayed at the feet of Jesus.

Questions

1. In what ways do you serve Christ?
2. Where can you strive to be more present at the "feet" of Christ's people?
3. What can you do to help protect and encourage others who strive to sit at the feet of Jesus?

Mark 14:27-31

Jesus said to them, "You will all falter in your faithfulness to me. It is written, I will hit the shepherd, and the sheep will go off in all directions. But after I'm raised up, I will go before you to Galilee."

Peter said to him, "Even if everyone else stumbles, I won't."

But Jesus said to him, "I assure you that on this very night, before the rooster crows twice, you will deny me three times."

But Peter insisted, "If I must die alongside you, I won't deny you." And they all said the same thing.

Application

- We always like to think that we are stronger than our peers. That even if everyone else does the wrong thing, we won't. That's what Peter thought, and Jesus told him differently. The situation changed, and Peter wasn't ready for it. But God is faithful, even when we aren't.

Questions

1. Have you ever done something you were certain you'd never do?
2. What changed?

CPSIA information can be obtained
at www.ICGtesting.com
Printed in the USA
LVOW01s0055190417
531284LV00004BA/6/P